We like ice cream

This book belongs to

_____

Written by Stephen Barnett
Illustrated by Rosie Brooks

Contents

About this book

Presenting experiences familiar to the child, the storylines and their illustrations will encourage reading and the expansion of the child's vocabulary as they seek to find out what happens next.

The broken window

My brother David and I
were playing catch in the
garden.

We threw the ball
to each other.

Then David threw the ball
too high.

The ball went over my
head, up and up.

It hit the window and
the window broke!

Our father came to see
what had happened.

We said that we are
sorry. We watched
while Dad cleaned up
the broken glass.

Now we go down to the end of the garden to throw the ball.

No more broken
windows!

We like ice cream

I like ice cream.

Do you like ice cream?

I like . . .

pink ice cream.

I like pink ice cream,

when the ice cream is
cold,

and when the day is hot!

The lost kite

We are flying our kite,

high up in the sky.

The kite is so high

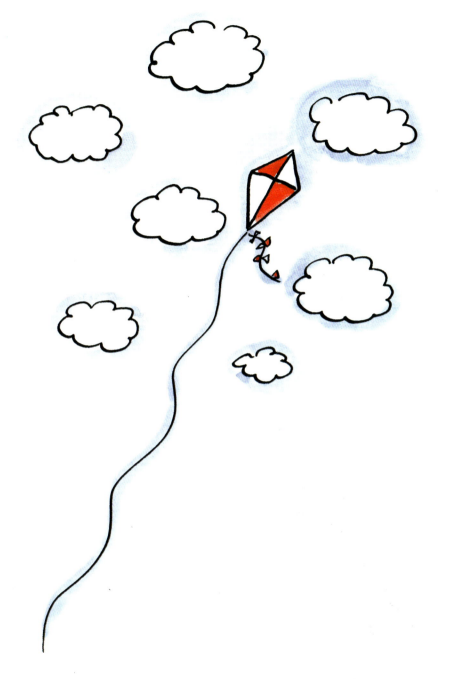

it looks very, very small.

Birds fly around the kite.

It almost touches the
clouds.

When the wind blows
hard,

the string breaks and the
kite flies away.

We take the rest of the string home. Tomorrow we will make a new kite!

New words

almost	new
blow	other
broke	over
catch	pink
clean	rest
cloud	sorry
cold	string
each	then
end	threw
glass	tomorrow
happen	too
hard	touch
head	watch
high	what
hit	wind
hot	window
like	

What did you learn?

The broken window
How was the window broken?
What is the brother's name?
Where do they play ball now?

We like ice cream
What ice cream colour does the girl like?
Do you like ice cream?

The lost kite
How many birds are flying around the kite?
What is the colour of the kite?
How many children are flying the kite?